D1146090

Things A Man Should Know

ABOUT STYLE

Things A Man Should Know
ABOUT STYLE

Scott Omelianuk
& Ted Allen

PRION

This edition published in 2001 by
Prion Books Limited, Imperial Works,
Perren Street, London NW5 3ED

Copyright © Hearst Communications, Inc.,
Hearst magazine Division, Publisher of *Esquire* Magazine (US)

Photographs by Brian Velenchenko
Styling by Severin and Louise Godwin
for Tiffany Whitford, NYC

ISBN 1-85375-441-2

Printed and bound in China by Everbest Printing Company

Introduction

What you don't know could fill a book, wiser men than we have said. And here it is. That book, we mean.

It should come as some small satisfaction to note that it's not all that big a book. It's also an amusing and pleasurable volume, we hope—something that might yield a quote or two for cocktail parties, or give you reason to chuckle quietly to yourself while riding on an airplane. But a book, nonetheless.

For while there are surely many endeavours about which you are a genuine expert—brilliant, even, at the absolute tip-top of your game, yessir—surely a man as assured as yourself would be the first to admit that there are certain areas about which you do not, as they say, know jack. This is true of all men.

When it comes to, say, 200-thread-count sheets or glass-blowing or piano bars, this ignorance is not only trivial, it's to be admired. But when it comes to dressing well and comporting yourself with style, it *is* a problem, and you know it. It can cost you jobs, women, and friends; it can cause you to be scorned by a maitre d', ignored by an airline-ticket agent, passed up by a taxi driver, and—perhaps worst of all—mocked behind your back by people who actually do know how to match a sock to a shoe to a suit. It can cause you to feel like less of a man than you are, and life is too short to feel like that.

We believe it was Sergio Valente who once said, "How you look tells the world how you feel"— a flimsy, pop-sociological aphorism that could have been spawned only by the seventies, but one that is nevertheless entirely correct. (It should be noted, however, that if you're still wearing Sergio Valente, you're telling the world that you feel like Huggy Bear; the pimp.)

What follows are simple nuggets of truth, lore, exhortation, and caution. These principles do not pretend to comprise the be-all, end-all encyclopaedia of matters sartorial. Rather, they are meant as guidelines—basic rules of the road, if you will. Some of which may even be broken, so long as you know what you're doing. Which you don't. Though you will.

David Granger
Editor in Chief, *Esquire* (US)

A man in a good suit and tie looks chic;
a man in a good suit without a tie looks more chic.

A man who uses the word "chic"
had better be kidding around.

Jeans must never meet an iron.

There is no foot pain so severe, no dress
shoe so fragile, no commute so arduous
as to justify the sartorial holocaust that is
wearing trainers with a suit.

At a pinch, paper clips can be used
in place of collar bones.

**At a pinch, paper clips cannot be used
in place of missing spectacle screws.**

That's why you have an extra pair of glasses.

Suits are cooler than sports jackets.
And give a short man the illusion of height.

A three-piece suit can make you look
slimmer, or bulkier, depending on the
pattern and whether it is tailored correctly.

Never button the bottom button on a waistcoat.

No, no one really knows why.

Well, it's either because (a) the waistcoat's first advocate, Edward VII, left his undone, either inadvertently or because he was fat,
or (b) the original full-length waistcoat had to be unbuttoned at the bottom to facilitate walking.

If you are one of those men who tends to whistle while prowling the halls at work with your hands jammed into your trouser pockets and jingling the coins therein, stop it.

Unless you want to look lumpy, reduce to an absolute minimum the number and size of the items you carry in your pockets.

Sergio Valente put it best when he said,
"How you look tells the world how you feel."

If you're still wearing Sergio Valente,
you look sort of like Huggy Bear.

With the possible exception of an
American Ivy League football game during
which people are shouting "boolah boolah"
and "twenty-three skidoo", it is never,
ever acceptable for a person of the male
persuasion to wear a fur coat—not
raccoon, not fox, not mink.

Certain men's coats, however, can tolerate having
their collars trimmed in a short, subdued fur.

Patchwork rabbit does not qualify as subdued.

The trenchcoat, while an excellent raincoat and quite versatile at a pinch, is not a proper winter topcoat.

The Chesterfield coat is.

When you buy a trenchcoat: The Burberry.

Sheepskin coats are fine, if a little cowboyish, which brings us to the next subject:

Cowboy boots: No.

Cowboy hats: No.

Cowboy shirts: Probably not.

Large belt buckles: Only if you're a cowboy.

P.S. Don't leave that bootlace tie
in your dresser drawer.

You could die.

Someone could find it.

Wearing a suit does not make you "a suit".

Wearing a bad suit or an incorrectly tailored suit or the same damned striped navy suit every day does.

The good suit: Horn buttons, hand-stitched lapels, felt under the collar, canvas interlining (stitched, not glued, in place), and a fabric soft enough to wear for twelve hours without making you itch to take your trousers off.

There are no bargains.

A custom-made suit is called "bespoke"
because it has been ordered, or spoken for,
by the customer.

Everyone should own
at least one bespoke suit.

Given that bespoke suits take two months to
make and can cost five grand and really aren't all
that much better than an expensive, high-quality
shop-bought suit, there's no need to own more
than one.

That one suit should be navy, black,
or dark grey, and solid.

Because it took two months to make and cost
five grand—you need to be able to wear it often
and with everything.

Centre vent: All-American.

Ventless: Italian, and not for
the prodigiously buttocked.

Side vents: Rather English. Quite.

Fabrics for easy-travelling suits:
Nailhead, crepe, tweed.

Fabrics for hot days: Cotton, linen, seersucker.

Seersucker: Not to be worn by men under
fifty or whose primary residence isn't
immediately adjacent to the county
courthouse in a US Southern state.

Maximum number of inches that the waist of new trousers can be taken in before the back pockets begin to meet: Two.

Gold buttons are not a necessary precondition for a jacket to be worn as a blazer.

In fact, gold buttons are never necessary, Admiral.

When the exchange rate is right, it can be cheaper to buy a plane ticket, fly to Italy, and buy two suits there than to buy them at home. Plus, you get to go to Italy.

Other things to buy in Italy: Florentine leather goods, Pinader stationery, Acqua di Parma cologne, and, the height of style, a really cool Vespa.

Not all Florentine leather goods are good.

All Vespas, however, are really cool.

Cigars are never stylish
in mixed company.

Smoking, while often fatal, offers many opportunities for the expression of style, notably Zippo lighters.

Do not ostentatiously light everyone else's cigarette all the time. They know how.

Never hold a cigarette between your thumb and index finger, with the palm up. Nazis do that.

Style affectations: Cigarette case, pince-nez, hip flask, walking stick.

Should you see a man with a walking stick, seize it and smack him on the hip flask with it.

Number of ties you *must* own: One.

Which one? The black knit tie.

A black knit tie coordinates with jeans and a blazer as well as it does with a French cuffed shirt and a custom-made suit.

Of course, you're better off with a handful,
all in silk: A couple of dark solids, a handful
of simple diagonal stripes, and one or two
natty small-patterned numbers, such as
you'd buy at Hermés.

Woven silk ties generally look more luxurious
than printed silk.

The Moscow theory as applied to tie acquisition:
Any time you see a tie you like, buy it. If you
decide to wait and come back later, it will be gone.

The tie pin is to fashion as the
appendix is to anatomy: Vestigial.

Hats will make a comeback some day.
It is not that day.

Paisley, too, will be back,
but you could ignore it.

Fanny packs are unacceptable,
if only because they are called "fanny packs".

Baseball caps are for getting the morning
paper. And for baseball.

Thermal headbands keep your ears and fore-head warm without messing up your hair or making you look the way you look when you wear earmuffs.

Unless you live in Chicago or Buffalo or International Falls, Minnesota, you must never wear a headband.

Ditto earmuffs.

Button-fly trousers are harder to fasten, but easier to unfasten.

To that end: Levi's jeans.

Polar fleece is for exercising and snow-shovelling and—let us not forget—is manufactured from recycled plastic bottles.

Polar fleece, while just as warm and at times just as soft as cashmere, will never be as desirable as cashmere.

Better than cashmere: Vicuna, which is woven of fibres combed from the chins of llamalike animals living in the Andes, and runs about £2,000 a square yard.

Dress-Down Friday does not excuse the visibility of chest hair.

The best thing about Dress-Down Friday is that
it makes those who decline to observe it
look really, really good.

Jack Kennedy wore polo shirts with suit jackets.

> Jack Kennedy knew *when* to
> wear polo shirts with suit jackets.

Good for Dress-Down Friday: Clark's desert boots.

Bad for Dress-Down Friday: Moon boots.

Sixty-pound shoes last half as long as £120 shoes, but £250 shoes will last you your whole life.

Two-hundred-and-fifty-pound shoes will not last your whole life if you break their backs by refusing to use a shoehorn.

Two-hundred-and-fifty-pound shoes without a shine can look like £60 shoes.

Women notice shoes.

They also notice nose hair; so should you.

Shoe size matters most at the ball of your foot, not at the toe (where it's OK for the shoe to be slightly too big), because the ball is where both your foot and the shoe bend.

Try on both the left and right shoe:
One foot is usually larger than the other.

Never try on shoes in the morning.

Try on shoes at midday.

Snakeskin shoes: No.

Crocodile shoes: Doubtful.

Crocodile shoes in any colour
other than black or brown:
Only if you're Barry White.

White shoes are for tennis.

Owning a set of golf clubs is not a licence for wearing hideous clothes.

Your glasses should match not only your face, but your clothing.

A guide: Match your glasses to your belt, your watch strap, and your shoes.

Of course, this gets pricey if you have a lot of different-coloured belts.

But, then: You need no belts in colours other than black and brown.

Silver, stainless steel, and chrome
watch straps go with everything.

Black or brown leather watch straps don't.

For those in the beginners' class—
Black shoes: Black strap, black belt.
Brown shoes: Brown strap, brown belt.

It was once considered vulgar for a gentleman to wear a watch, since he might appear overly concerned about the passing of time.

A real Timex is better than a fake Rolex.

The best Timex is the original: The Mercury.

The best leather coats are those made with the fewest, largest pieces of hide.

Trifold wallets bulge more than bifold wallets.

Far from attesting to vast wealth, a
bulging wallet attests to slovenliness.

After all, a really wealthy man lets
his accountant settle his bills.

Plus, a bulging wallet is uncomfortable
and bad for your trousers.

Straw hats are for Kentucky colonels and gardeners.

Clyde—of Bonnie and—was neither a colonel nor a gardener and wore a straw hat, and look what happened to him.

Argyle anything is fraught with peril.

What to do should anyone call you a "dandy": Open wardrobe. Remove contents. Begin again.

Wearing suits when you don't have to will cause people to think that you have really great suits or that you are really comfortable in suits, or that you are a Jehovah's Witness.

> Three-button suit: Yes.
> Two-button: Yes.
> One-button: Only on a tuxedo.

Speaking of buttons, with two you fasten only the top button; with three it's either the middle or the middle and the top.

Should you find yourself in a four-button suit coat: Unfasten all buttons. Remove. Discard.

A man, unless he is under the age of six,
should not wear dungarees.

You know how the outside pockets
of a new suit are stitched shut?
Leave them stitched shut.

This preserves the lean shape of a suit
by prohibiting you from stuffing the
pockets full of stuff.

A good suit treated well shouldn't be
dry-cleaned more than two or three times
a season; a good tuxedo treated well
should never be dry-cleaned.

Turn-ups: On suit trousers or any trousers you'd wear with a tie, except tuxedo trousers.

No turn-ups: On jeans and khakis, unless they are pleated, which they should never be.

Khakis, which are patterned like military trousers, should never be pleated because military trousers have no pleats and because Humphrey Bogart wore khakis and you can be damned sure his didn't have pleats.

The pleats of trousers that fit
properly will never bulge or gape
but will lie flat against your lap.

Contrary to popular belief, a quirky nonconformity
is not expressed through a Mickey Mouse watch
or a Bugs Bunny tie, because, well, do you know
how many tens of thousands of those things
sell each year?

Likewise, wit or humour should never be
expressed through your socks.

Once upon a time labels were worn
only on the inside of clothes.
Those were better times.

Some discreet logos, however, are tolerable on
sports clothing: Ralph Lauren's polo player and
pony, Lacoste's crocodile, Fred Perry's crest,
Brooks Brothers' golden fleece.

Umbrellas: Size matters.

While it is acceptable to carry one of those collapsible numbers in your briefcase for emergencies, a well-made, full-sized bumbershoot is a true mark of style.

With a wood handle.

And a sharp, dangerous point.

On the other hand, umbrellas are like fancy gloves: Eventually, you will lose them. Spend accordingly.

Blue jeans: Weekends.

Black jeans: Weekend nights.

White jeans: With those elf boots
you saved from the eighties.

See also stone-washed jeans—no,
actually, *don't* see stone-washed jeans.

**Unless you're a football star,
never wear anything with
your name or number on it.**

A goatee: No.

A soul patch: No.

Elvis sideburns: No.

A ponytail: You're joking, right?
Of course you're joking. Ha, ha.

Slim-fitting clothes are for slim men.

> Which means if you're a thirty-six,
> you won't look skinnier shoehorning
> yourself into a thirty-four. You'll
> look skinnier wearing a thirty-six.

Even at a company picnic, the boss
should never subject his employees
to a display of his knees.

The above rule doesn't apply if the boss is a she.

Speaking of shes: The great thing about buying a woman thong underwear is that you get to try it on, too.

That was a joke.

A briefcase is to a man as a handbag is to a woman.

If you wear mostly brown shoes, get a brown briefcase; if you wear mostly black shoes, get a black one.

Better: Have one of each.

Backpacks are for students and hikers.

A good leather briefcase cannot
be had for less than £300.

Better a good, nylon canvas portfolio
than a bad leather briefcase.

45

What's worse about a bad briefcase
is the cheap hardware, which will
scratch and break.

The quality briefcase: Full-grain leather, inside
and out; brass hardware; strong locks;
strong, leather strap (when applicable).

Be forewarned: Using an attaché's strap
will cause shiny spots on the shoulders
of your suit jackets.

Unless you have something to hide or happen to
be Des Lynam, you look exactly half as attractive
with a moustache.

Go to work clean-shaven because you are not
Sonny Crockett and even if you are, *Miami Vice*
was cancelled in 1989.

Things to shave: Face, head.

Things not to shave: everything else.

If you have a lot of back hair,
you could have it waxed.
Or you could keep your shirt on.

Generally, everybody should keep his shirt on.

Under no circumstances sing the song
"I'm Too Sexy". Not alone. Not in groups.
And particularly not while dressing in
front of a mirror.

**Toupees and comb-overs
betray a level of moral dishonesty
equivalent to the practice of
buttock augmentation.**

If you are going bald,
cut your hair close to the scalp.

Despite the wickedly clever strategies developed by department stores to market such items each holiday season, do not succumb to purchasing a Christmas tie.

Nor a Christmas sweater.

Nor—especially nor—clothing
that emits Christmas music.

Likewise there is little reason to wear green on St Patrick's Day: Red, white, and blue on the Queen's birthday: Or orange at Halloween.

Socks with sandals and dark socks
with shorts are statements to be avoided.

Sandals?
On the beach.
In the backyard.

Flat or waxed shoelaces stay tied far better than
round unwaxed ones.

All but the very best dress shoes
now come with round unwaxed laces.
You should replace the laces on those that don't.

Men with pale ankles should
always wear socks.

Men with ankles, period, should
always wear socks.

Men who refuse to wear socks should be
prepared for the consequences of exuding
the heady aroma of a locker room.

Exempt from the above: Italian men
or men who look Italian enough to
have that certain something that allows
them to wear clothes that no normal man
can wear without provoking laughter.

Besides, your feet will feel cooler
if you wear socks.

Because socks wick away moisture better
than leather, that's why.

The length of one's sideburns is
inversely proportional to one's ability
to rise in the corporate hierarchy.

Unless one works at Graceland.

Shaving is important not only to make you look clean, but so as to avoid sandpapering the face of the person you kiss.

Shaving does not require so much foam that your face resembles a meringue pie.

Shaving is best done in the shower or immediately thereafter.

Shaving is never done with her razor.

　　　　More important: Her shaving is
　　　　never done with *your* razor.

Hide it if you must.

　　　　Special attention: Just under your nostrils.
　　　　Just under your lower lip.
　　　　Between your eyebrows.

Acquire a styptic pencil, which won't stick
to your face all the way to work the way
those bits of toilet paper do.

Wear no clothing emblazoned with opinions or exhortations.

If you own any T-shirts with such legends as
"I'm with Stupid" or "100% Bitch" or
"Nobody Knows Me Like Cosmo",
please put this book down and back away slowly.

It is far better to arrive at an event overdressed
than underdressed—if you leave early, people will
think you've got somewhere more important to go.

A freshly pressed linen suit doesn't look nearly as good as one that's been worn fourteen times without ever encountering an iron.

The business-shirt wardrobe:
Though some style books would prescribe four white shirts, four blue shirts, etc., it's better to have whatever kind of high-quality shirts you like that are acceptable in your office.

That said, your shirt wardrobe should total at least ten, so that the first five can be in the laundry for a week before you're caught without.

Not all shirt collar styles suit all men.

Long face: spread collar,
button-down collar, tab collar.

Square face: button-down collar,
rounded-point collar.

Round face: button-down collar, long-point collar.

Oval face: anything but the rounded collar.

Collarless shirts make you look either
stupid or like a priest or like a stupid priest.

The business-shoe wardrobe: You can't go
wrong with one pair of plain-toe oxfords in
black, one cap-toe or wing tip in black, and
one plain-toe or wing tip in brown.

Oxfords is a fancy name for lace-up shoes.

Loafers, which are descended from Indian
moccasins and shoes sewn by Norwegian
fisherman to wear at sea, are too casual to
be worn with business suits.

They are excellent casual shoes, however.

And not bad if you're cruising the
North Sea for salmon.

Shoe styles in descending order of dressiness: formal pumps, plain-toe oxfords, cap-toe oxfords, wing tip or patterned leather oxfords, loafers, espadrilles, Dr Scholl's sandals, waders, oily rags.

Speaking of espadrilles, if you wear them, you should feel ashamed.

Or French. And ashamed.

No matter what fond memories they evoke of
the first time he wore them, there are certain
garments from a man's past that he should never
seek to wear again: a thin leather tie, rainbow-
coloured braces, those little underwear
briefs with cartoon superheroes printed on them.

In fact, wear no funny underwear.

Funny underwear shall be defined as those
garments including, but not limited to,
neon-coloured briefs, boxers printed with
lipstick kisses, or any style of skivvies
whose fly zone is emblazoned with the phrase
"Home of the Whopper".

For those still contemplating the wearing of funny underwear, think: When you are removing your trousers for the viewing pleasure of another, do you really want that person to laugh?

Unpolished shoes are the bloodstained hands of style.

Unpolished shoes?
OK, then, how about uncombed hair,
unshaven face, untrimmed nostrils,
unbrushed teeth, unwiped...
do we need to go on?

Cleanly trimming your fingernails
is mandatory.

Having a manicure is acceptable.

Finishing your nails with any kind
of polish is something Liberace
would have done and is, like most
matters of style pertaining to the
late pianist, unacceptable.

No man should dye his hair.

For all hairstyling products: A little dab will, indeed, do you.

In the unlikely event that a little dab will not do you, get a different hairstyle.

Your hairstyle should require no more time to complete than it does for you to tie your shoes.

When in doubt, go short.

One reason short hair is better: Easy styling.

Another reason short hair is better:
Less susceptible to "hat hair".

Yet a third reason short hair is better:
You needn't shampoo until it begins to smell.

That was a joke, too.

Problem with short hair:
Frequent haircuts are essential.

Solution: Get frequent haircuts.

A suggestion: Every time you get a haircut,
before you leave, make an appointment for
another haircut, generally four weeks later.

If you favour barbers over salons—
and you are to be commended for this—
find one that will shave the back of your
neck with hot lather.

Using very hot water to wash your face causes
your pores to open and moisture loss to ensue.

Plus it hurts.

Too much cologne is to style as big hair is to style as platform shoes are to style as padded underwear is to style, which is to say way too much.

What is too much cologne? More than two squirts of good cologne, or more than zero squirts of cheap cologne.

Cologne is applied not to the face (that's after-shave) but sprayed on the chest, the back of the neck, the hair, or the hairy part of your forearms.

The reason for putting cologne in those places is that hair is the best carrier for scent.

Good mouthwash is overpriced,
but cheap mouthwash is useless.

Breath mints. Not gum.

Tooth-bleaching should be
left to the professionals.

There should be only one toothpaste flavour in your medicine cabinet: Mint.

As essential as your toothbrush,
which is to say, an absolute must:
A nose-hair trimmer.

If this doesn't seem to apply to you now,
give it time—it will.

It can also be used in the ear.

If this doesn't seem to apply to you now,
give it time—it will.

73

The morning shower is as much about therapy as it is about cleanliness.

Lather. Rinse. Don't repeat. The repeat part is just the shampoo company's attempt to get you to run out of shampoo sooner.

Expensive shampoo smells really good.

Deodorant/antiperspirant, not just deodorant.

Let your deodorant dry for a few seconds before putting on your shirt.

There is no substitute for thick, luxurious, large, high-quality, 100 per cent cotton bath towels.

The convention for monogramming towels:
The first letter of her first name, then the first letter of their last name, then the first letter of his first name, such that if a woman named Amy were to marry Steven Spielberg, the monogram would be...
Must we spell it out for you?

Leave enough room in your wardrobe so that your suits and shirts hang freely without touching.

Hang suits from shaped wooden hangers.

This prevents a suit's lapels from rolling in on themselves and creasing.

If you haven't worn it in the last year, get rid of it.

Do not allow children or pets to enter your
wardrobe.

> As you contemplate tattooing yourself or
> piercing body parts, try to remember a
> single T-shirt you bought at a rock concert
> five years ago that you still wear.

George Clooney didn't look as good with
that Caesar haircut as he thought he did.

The gym is no place to be fashion conscious.

To that end: Shorts or tracksuit bottoms, not
tights.

Dress for the job you want, not the job you have.

A case where the above rule should be ignored: When the job you have is the chief loan officer at a very conservative bank, and the job you want is to be Mookie, the dancing woodchuck, in a musical adaptation of George Orwell's *Animal Farm*.

If you're not sure whether or not it
looks good on you, it doesn't.

        The black cashmere turtleneck
        looks good on everyone.

Also: The grey flannel suit.

No level of fitness justifies
wearing a tank top in public.

**No level of fitness—or,
for that matter, drunkenness—
justifies wearing a tank top at home.**

A plain short-sleeved T-shirt
works perfectly well at the gym.

While travelling, two small suitcases
are better than one large one.

While two small suitcases are better than one
large one, one small suitcase is even better.

Best of all:
A Sherpa to carry everything for you.

Stylish luggage is great, but, before you spend a mint, consider what will happen to it after you check in, and know that baggage handlers give special attention to buttery-soft leather only because it suggests valuable and easily fencible goods inside.

Travel essential: Mouthwash. Especially on overnight flights.

At the dry-cleaner: Order your shirts on hangers, unless you're travelling, in which case boxed, folded shirts are handy.

Pack each suit and dress shirt on
individual hangers and in individual
plastic bags from the dry-cleaner:
The slippery plastic reduces creasing.

Or, roll clothing rather than folding it,
because each fold is a potential crease.

The best travel suit: "High-twist" wool or wool
crepe, which barely creases and smooths
instantly in a steam-filled bathroom.

Lycra, when used sparingly:
Not just for aerobics classes any more.

Besides offering comfort and stretch,
small amounts of Lycra help garments
hold their shape and resist creases.

The correct Lycra proportions: Shirts made of 95
per cent cotton and 5 per cent Lycra. Suits made
of 99 per cent wool and 1 per cent Lycra.

The two-day business trip: One solid blue suit, one pair of grey wool trousers, one black belt, one pair of black cap-toes, one pair of casual shoes, three versatile ties, two white dress shirts and one blue or grey, three pairs of black socks, three changes of underwear, lightweight tan sweater, lined raincoat.

Roll up two of those ties. Pack them in your shoes—the ones you're not wearing. Wear the other tie on the plane.

The weekend getaway: One sports jacket, one pair of dress trousers, one button-down oxford, light sweater, knit tie, swimming trunks, tennis togs, casual shoes, trainers.

The plain getaway: Jeans, shirt, trainers, false moustache and glasses.

If you wear a suit on a plane and there
is a flight delay or cancellation, the ticket
agent will help you in a way that she
wouldn't if you were in a tracksuit.

The preceding principle also applies to the
following situations: At restaurants, in certain
nightclubs, taxi-hailing, when being pulled over by
a policeman, when shopping for lingerie (unless
it's for yourself), and in the office, either for the
bossing about of a subordinate or the receiving of
a bossing about from a superior.

Be not just polite but charming to ticket
agents, desk clerks, waiters, bellboys.

On a two-week holiday, be sure that
there are laundry facilities at the end of
week one, then pack exactly half as much
as you otherwise would have.

Travel essentials: Gaviscon, Nurofen,
and melatonin—if you can get it—which will
help you sleep in an unfamiliar time zone.

Travel inessentials:
Gas-X, Ex-Lax, and Anusol.

If you need those things, pal, you shouldn't
be going anywhere.

Always stay in the kind of hotel
that will lend you an umbrella,
should you need one.

Always stay in the kind of hotel that will
press a shirt instantly, any time, day or night.

Always stay in the kind of hotel
that will bring you a newspaper
with your room-service breakfast.

For the same reason you tip the barman
for the first round, tip the housekeeper
on the first day.

A suede blazer is acceptable, if risky
(no bootlace tie, no boots, no ten-gallon hat).

A leather blazer is not, except when you've been
asked to whack somebody with Joe Pesci.

The Hawaiian shirt: No.

It's acceptable, if you're old, to dress in a way
that makes you appear younger.

It's not acceptable, if you're old, to dress in a
way that makes you appear younger than twelve.

Wearing a sports watch with a suit makes you appear younger.

Wearing trainers with a suit makes you appear younger than twelve.

Or like a stand-up comedian.

Which brings us to Al Gore.
Even he shouldn't wear a watch
with a built-in calculator.

Button-downs, because of their
informal roots, should never be
worn with a double-breasted suit.

Button-downs are best worn with a sports jacket.

You know how some men wear a shirt with a tie
and the shirt's a little too small so their neck
sort of curls out over the collar like the end of
a German sausage bursting beyond its casing?
Don't do that.

Unless you speak with a French accent and sing
"Thank Heaven for Little Girls", your wedding day
is the only appropriate day to wear a buttonhole.

A black suit with a crisp white straight-collar shirt (not a button-down) and a long solid black tie can be worn to any event where you're requested to wear a tuxedo.

That said, never exercise the option of black tie optional.

Likewise, black tie is not the sort of dress with which to get "creative".

When in doubt, wear black.

On the other hand, wearing all black, all the time, is the transparent affectation of people who want to be seen as artsy, and who should just quit it.

Though many claim that suits and ties inhibit creativity, it's instructive to remember that Matisse and Einstein did just fine in them.

A suit is not an obligation:
It is your protector.

A tie is not an obligation:
It is an opportunity.

Although the preceding two items have the ring of New Age bullshit, the point is don't shirk the suit and tie.

Despite their prevalence in country clubs, boat shoes should not be worn with a navy blazer, Biff.

Skinny men can wear things
fat men cannot.

Italian men, even fat Italian men,
can wear things English men cannot.

Tall black men can wear things
tall white men cannot.

A man wears nothing under his kilt.

Which is why a man
should never wear a kilt.

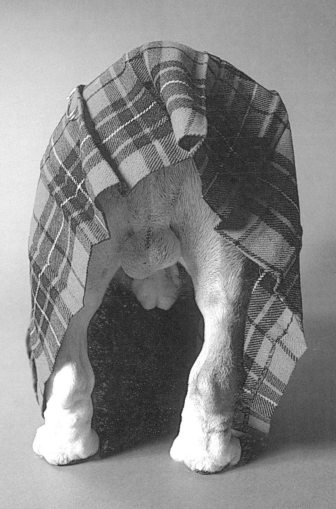

Brown suits, while wearable, are touch and go.

Saying that brown is the new black is like
saying chocolate is the new vanilla.

People who say that brown is the new black tend
to work in the fashion industry, which abhors the
idea of clothing that "never goes out of style".

There will never be a new black.

Contrary to popular belief,
not everybody looks better in black.

To wit: Tall, thin men of exceptionally
pale visage look more dead than better.

Green suits are not wearable,
are difficult to match ties to,
and can cause a short man to
be mistaken for a leprechaun.

Short men need the illusion of height, which
means: Dark suits, vertical lines, tapered trousers,
two- as opposed to three-button suits, and the
avoidance of the horizontal effect of pocket flaps
and trousers with turn-ups.

Tall, thin men need the illusion of breadth, which means: Plaids, patterns, thick, non-clingy fabrics, looser three-button suits, wider lapels, flapped pockets, trousers with turn-ups.

Ties with vertical stripes: No.

Fat men: See short men. Plus, seek jackets with only slightly padded shoulders to avoid the appearance of tightness there; avoid bulky tweeds, vivid patterns, and pinstripes, which, like the grid on a globe, only serve to accentuate rotundity.

Similarly, avoid stripes on tight-fitting shorts, unless it is your intention to delineate the longitude and latitude of your Mercator projection.

100

No man, not even a figure skater,
should wear sequins.

No man, not even a polo player,
should wear jodhpurs.

No man, not even a scoutmaster,
should wear garters.

Rent no clothing.

Lend no clothing.

Borrow no clothing.

Especially your wife's.

Braces, ill-employed, produce wedgies.

When to wear braces without a suit or tie:
When you are Robin Williams.

Use of a pocket handkerchief generally indicates a sophisticated level of dressing, so long as that handkerchief wasn't bought in a boxed set with a matching tie.

Should you be put off by fluffy-looking, colourful handkerchiefs, or should you not wish to have another colour and pattern to worry about matching with your suit, tie, and shirt, opt for a white linen hanky, and fold it squarely, such that a half-inch shows from your breast pocket. Presto.

If you can slip two fingers between your neck and the buttoned collar of a new dress shirt, the shirt will fit comfortably after laundering.

To avoid turning your collar into a garrotte:
Light starch.

The shirt placket, the belt buckle,
and the trouser fly should all line up.

The shirt placket: The strip of material
sewn to the front of your shirt through
which buttons are fastened.

Speaking of belt buckles,
the point of your tie should never fall below it.

Ties decorated with golf tees or with the paintings of dead rock musicians coordinate with nothing.

It is never acceptable to loosen your tie, except during the process of its removal.

Loosen your tie by gently working free the knot, rather than pulling the end through the knot, which stretches out your tie.

You are in your car an hour a day;
you are in your clothes from morning to night.
Spend accordingly.

The seat-belt shoulder strap
goes under your tie.

Good shoes and a good haircut
matter more than a great suit.

You can't smoke a pipe
if you're under forty-five.

You can't wear a fedora
if you're under forty-five.

You can't wear a bow tie with
anything other than a tuxedo if
you're under forty-five or not a
famous novelist or not a total geek.
Got that, professor?

Still, you need to know how to
tie a bow for formal events,
like your wedding.

The best way to master the tying of a bow tie:
Get someone who knows how to teach you and
then practise incessantly.

This you should do weeks before the day
you actually need to tie it.

On that day, keep a clip-on in reserve,
should your bow-tying skills fail,
which they probably will.

Clip-on ordinary ties are perfectly
acceptable for gentlemen, but only
for those still at primary school.

Very few people want to see you in
cycling shorts, and those who do
might not be your target audience.

Likewise tight,
black leather pants, Mr Bon Jovi.

Never allow yourself to be seen
with anyone employing a fan,
a beret, a monocle, or spats.

If he's got all four, run and hide.

Silk shirts: No.

Diaphanous shirts: No.

Blousy pirate shirts: Unless you're a figure skater. And even then—actually, especially then—no.

Glittery clothing: No.

Knickers: No.

Monograms: Proceed with caution.

> If you must monogram shirts,
> do it only on the waist, below
> the breast pocket or on the front left tail.

And never forget: Clothing emblazoned with
crests is to be avoided by anyone who isn't a
member of the Royal family or Captain Stubing
from *The Love Boat*.

Select at your peril glasses so distinctive and prominent that they become your primary feature.

Case in point: Swifty Lazar, Elton John, Dame Edna Everage, Christopher Biggins.

Round face: Square glasses.
Long face: Round glasses.

Sunglasses not only prevent you from squinting (which can eventually result in unwanted wrinkles) but protect you from cataracts.

The reason celebrities wear sunglasses indoors is not because you would otherwise recognize them, which they've long grown accustomed to, but so they don't readily notice *you* recognizing them.

Unless the burden of celebrity is a daily pox upon your life, do not wear sunglasses indoors.

A £150 shirt will look like
a £15 shirt if it is professionally
laundered instead of hand-washed.

Still, ironing correctly is difficult and tedious
and best left to experts.

There is no such thing as a stylish slipper.

Velvet slippers with gold brocade—unless
you're over fifty and incredibly wealthy and
feel comfortable in a cravat and are hosting a
jazz-age cotillion in your city home, as opposed
to your various country and island homes: No.

No one should feel comfortable wearing a cravat.

It follows that there is no use for a tie pin.

Ditto for a dickie.

No, a dickie is the neck part of a turtleneck sweater without the sweater part, which one wears under another shirt to give the impression that one is wearing an entire turtleneck sweater.

Yes, a dickie *is* a stupid thing.

You will be happiest if you regard dress shirts as ultimately disposable.

Before you buy one more shirt, get a tailor to measure these portions of your person, and commit the numbers to memory: Neck, arms, chest.

Other numbers to remember: Half an inch of shirt collar above the jacket collar, half an inch of shirt cuff, one-and-a-half inches of trouser turn up, two inches more belt than inches on your actual waist.

Despite its presence on the label of every high-quality shirt (and many cheap ones besides), only a few insiders know what "single-needle tailoring" is.

Single-needle tailoring: Seams stitched down the outside of a shirt first and then from the inside, using one needle and forming a lock-stitch, which is stronger and prevents the puckering that comes with faster, cheaper, double-needle stitching.

You are now at liberty to forget you've ever heard of "single-needle tailoring".

Cotton/polyester blended shirts don't breathe, do pucker at the seams, and will "bobble" after a few launderings.

"Easy-care" is for those who don't.

One definition of the high-quality shirt: 100 per cent cotton, or 95 per cent cotton and 5 per cent Lycra.

Another definition of the high-quality shirt: A "split yoke", signified by a vertical seam between the shoulder blades, which permits custom shirt makers to adjust the fit of each shoulder separately.

Yet a third definition of the high-quality shirt: Small, tight stitches, removable collar bones, a button on the cuff placket, pleats on the sleeve where it enters the cuff, well-sewn buttons with an extra one attached to the inside of the shirt tail.

One ring, maximum. On a finger.
Nothing Masonic.

Silver or platinum or white gold,
not yellow gold.

Harrison Ford doesn't look as good with
that earring as he thinks he does.

David Beckham doesn't look as good with
that earring as he thinks he does.

Captain Hook—all right, on *him*,
the earring looks good.

Karl Lagerfeld doesn't look as good
with that fan, those sunglasses,
that trench coat, that make-up,
that cigarette holder, or that ponytail
as he thinks he does.

The only good tattoo is a very, very small
tattoo placed where no one can see it—
which is to say, why get one?

A man in a suit without a tie
can get away with wearing loafers:
A man in a suit with a tie cannot.

Cheap cashmere is less soft and more fragile
than expensive wool.

Number of goats that sacrifice their belly
hairs for your cashmere sweater: Six.

Jumpers: Solids, not argyles,
unless you're off to Andover.

If you must wear patterned, which carries
grave risks, they must be patterned on the
back as well as the front.

A T-shirt that shows through a dress shirt
is the male equivalent of the visible panty line.

Once more: Do not wear button-down collars with double-breasted suits.

Do not unbutton double-breasted suits
as David Letterman always does.

Think twice about double-breasted suits.

The only thing worse than wearing socks that don't cover one's calves is wearing patterned socks that don't cover one's calves.

If you lose one cuff link,
remove the remaining orphan;
this will make it look like
you've omitted them on purpose
and have insouciant personal style.

Keep a lint roller in your office. And your car.

Also for your office: A small safety pin, a large safety pin, a sewing kit, a small bottle of spot remover.

The button-down collar, left unbuttoned: No.

> Unless you're wearing it with a pair of
> jeans or khakis and without a tie, in
> which case it should never be starched
> or ironed, either.

Always keep a fresh shirt, laundered and
pressed, and a tie in your office.

> Never take a tie to a dry cleaner.
> who will invariably ruin it.

For formal affairs:
Buy the lightest-weight tuxedo you can find,
because dancing and drinking and scantily clad
women cause such events to become overheated.

Dancing can be hell on your clothes,
your shoes, and your hairstyle.

Dancing is best performed by those who can dance.

Those who can dance know who they are.
Usually.

That said, if she asks, dance you must.

What you find at a factory outlet store is what other people refused to buy or what some marketing director thinks you will buy because you're the kind of person who shops at a factory outlet store.

Khakis worn religiously on Friday are no less a uniform than a business suit worn the previous four days.

Nonetheless, you can never have too many khakis. Or heavyweight white T-shirts. For Saturday.

Your belt and shoes should match
in colour, if not material.

Speaking of colour,
there is little use for pink,
peach or teal.

It's not the name on the label or the amount on the credit card receipt, but how good you look in it.

One £600 suit is a better investment than two £300 suits.

Of course, clothes are not really "investments" because, unlike a Jackson Pollock or stock shares, they cannot appreciate. They're clothes.

It's more important to a man's daily life
to have a good tailor than a good doctor.

How to pick a tailor:
Visit the finest men's store in town, find the
best-dressed salesman in the suit department,
ask him where he goes. Then, visit another fine
men's store and run that tailor's name by the
best-dressed salesman there. Repeat.

How to talk to a good tailor: Present your taste in
cuffs, sleeve length, give at the waist, and roominess
in the seat; and then let him do what he wants.

Tip him generously.

At the tailor's, carry everything you normally
carry: Wallet, keys, Mace, etc.

Suit trousers ride on your waist—
about an inch below your navel—
not your hips, like jeans do.

Suit trousers should break on top
of your shoe, so that the crease on the leg
rumples just slightly.

If your suit trousers are too short, you'll
look like Garrison Keillor.

If your suit trousers are too long:
Charlie Chaplin.

Talented clothing salesmen are an essential part of selecting the right clothes, but finding such a man . . . Aye, there's the rub.

> Two elements of style that will outlast any man who is smart enough to own them:
> A sterling belt buckle from Tiffany & Co. and simple cuff links.

A restaurant meal tastes better when you're wearing a suit jacket.

> When wearing nice clothing in a restaurant, order only things that can be eaten neatly and with a fork.

Things that particularly do not qualify for the above: Soup. Spaghetti. Lobster. King crab claws.

Whether a tie is too fat or too skinny must be
decided by you alone, on a tie-by-tie basis.

When in doubt, ask a woman.

Know that she will often be wrong, too,
and that, ultimately, a man is adrift in a
vast sea of complexity and indecision
that he alone must ply.

Never trust a fashion magazine.

Solution for snags on many garments:
Don't cut the errant fibre; rather,
thread it on to a needle and pull it
through the snag so that it hangs on
the inside.

Never iron anything that could melt.

The presence or absence of gold stripes
on the lining of ties that once
attested to a tie's quality
no longer does so.

Testing a tie's quality:
Dangle it from the narrow blade
and see if it hangs without twisting;
pull from both ends and see if it
returns to its original size and shape:
Drape it over your arm and make sure
the narrow end is centred against the wide end.

Or you can follow this old maxim:
If it makes a good knot, it's a good tie.

A safe width for ties: Three and a half inches.

A safe length: Fifty-six inches.

It is no easier or more comfortable
to wear a sports jacket and trousers
than it is to wear a suit.

If the trousers you'd wear with the sports jacket
are more comfortable than the trousers with your
suit, you need a new suit.

Somewhere in Britain, people are
still wearing shell suits, and you
owe God your deepest thanks that
you have the presence of mind
not to be among them.

Hospital scrubs are an excellent
choice when your destination is
your bed and you are going
there alone.

Or if you are Dr Doug Ross.

An alternative: Sulka silk pyjamas.

Because you never know when Hef might call.

Wait—yeah, you do. Hef will never call, but have
you ever felt Sulka silk pyjamas? Mmmm.

The only people who can wear coloured shirts with white collars are obscenely overpaid CEOs and Donald Trump.

And even they look ridiculous in them, but who's going to tell them?

Wearing an orange tie will not make you look like Frank Sinatra.

Wearing an orange pocket handkerchief will not make you look like Frank Sinatra.

Frank Sinatra is dead. OK?

If you hang your jacket on a chair and then sit on the chair and lean back, your jacket will look as if you hung it on a chair and then sat on the chair and leaned back.

Drape your scarf on that chair and place that umbrella on the floor and you're going to find yourself buying another scarf and another umbrella very soon.

Fabric weights are the chemistry of style; wool trousers and a linen shirt or a flannel shirt with a silk tie are corrosive mixtures.

Jack Nicholson can wear two-tone gangster shoes only because he is Jack Nicholson.

Tom Wolfe can wear ice-cream-coloured suits only because he is Tom Wolfe.

And remember: Even Tom Wolfe has his bad days.

Before overindulging in combat pants, consider the stylistic endurance of loons.

144

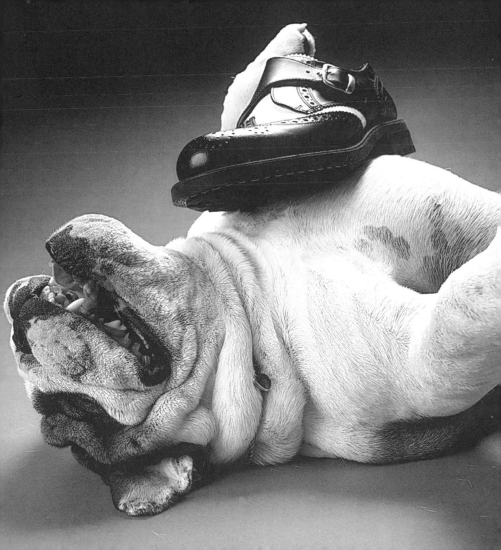

Clothing that reveals your preferences in sports teams and rock bands should be left at home with your parents when you move out.

Clothing that reveals your preferences in institutions of higher education is for jogging and car-washing.

Only professional drivers need driving gloves.

Observing Dress-Down Friday tells the world that you're only confident enough to wear what you're told you can wear.

On the other hand, we suppose that we are telling you what to wear, aren't we?

Dress-Down Friday was invented to embarrass well-dressed men.

Really well-dressed men are not affected by this.

Men named Chick tend to wear
shoes with stacked heels.

Shoes with stacked heels, like the name
Chick, are inappropriate for men.

Woven shoes are for men with small feet.

Think twice about woven shoes.

Plain-toe shoes make big feet look bigger
than do cap-toe shoes or wing tips.

Cowboy boots make big feet look bigger still. Plus they have stacked heels. Plus they're cowboy boots, for God's sake. And didn't we already tell you about cowboy boots?

Of course, plain-toe shoes aren't as bad as those big red floppy clown shoes, which make your feet look *really* big. But in a good way.

Don't attempt the tango in clown shoes, unless you are a trained professional.

If you are a tango professional, man, what on earth do you need our help for?

> If you are a tango professional, please donate this book to someone less well-endowed in the style department.

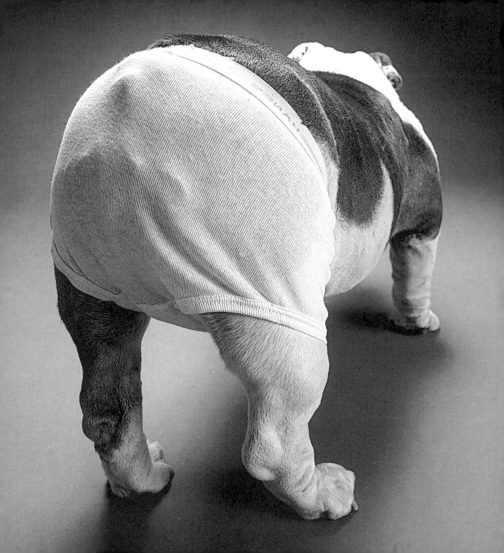

On planes, briefs are more comfortable than boxers, as contents may shift during flight.

Boxers: With roomy and pleated trousers.

Briefs: With jeans and tighter-cut trousers.

Bikini briefs: In the store, unbought.

To follow slavishly every new fashion trend because it is fashionable and trendy is to reveal a profound insecurity, and that is not what style is about.

At the end of the day—or, in this case, the book—know simply that you need only remember and bring to bear those style guidelines that work best for you.

Put another way:
To have absolute style
is to break absolute rules—
sometimes even these.